"It is as if we enhance our being if we can gain a place in the memory of others; it is a new life that we acquire, which becomes as precious to us as the one we received from Heaven."

- Montesquieu

ISBN: 9798682581818

How to use this journal

For family:

◘ The last two pages of the diary contain two empty spaces for custom questions - Write down two personal questions you would like to ask your grandparent.

For grandparents:

◘ Read all the questions part of the different sections once in advance.

◘ Take some time to reflect on your answers - sometimes memories need time to resurface.

◘ For each question, try to elaborate your answer as much as you can.

This journal contains memories and
life stories of

_____

A special dedication to:

Family Origins

Question 1

When and where were you born?

Tell me how it was like at that time and in that place

Question   2

Where did our family come from?

Tell me what you know about the earliest

history of the family

Question 3

Were any of our ancestors well known for anything?

Tell me about someone in the family that seemed to be a special character

Question 4

Was there ever any feud or dramatic

event in the wider family?

Tell me about any famous story that goes

around in the family

Question 5

Are there any family names or items that have been passed down from generation to generation?

Question 6

How did your parents meet and start a family?

Tell me about their background and what they were doing for a living

Question 7

What's your favorite memory of your parents?

Tell me your most cherished memory of your mother and of your father

Question 8

Did you have a favorite sibling?

Tell me about your relationship with your siblings, if you had any

Question 9

Did you have any cousin?

Tell me about your relationship with
your cousins, if you had any

Question 10

What were your own grandparents like?

Tell me something you remember about

any of your grandparents

Question 11

What family member were you closest to?

Tell me about someone in your family

with whom you had a special connection

Question   12

What family tradition did we carry on?

Tell me about any custom or habit you

have inherited from your family

Childhood

Question 13

Where did you grow up?

Tell me about your childhood home

Question 14

What were you like as a child?

Tell me how you looked and what kind of

things you liked doing

Question 15

What is your favorite childhood memory?

Tell me one of the memories you cherish

the most from that time

Question 16

Did you have any pets?

Did you like animals in general?

Question 17

Who was your best friend?

Tell me about childhood friends who were closest to you

Question 18

What games would you play with your friends?

Tell me what things you enjoyed doing most with your friends

Question 19

What was your favorite toy?

Tell me about any hobbies or special item

you had as a kid

Question 20

Did you enjoy school?

Tell me how it was like going to school at that time

Question 21

Were you a difficult or well behaved child?

Tell me about your character and personality as a child

Question 22

How did you spend the summer holidays?

Tell me about any particular memory of a

summer vacation

Question   23

Who was your role model?

Tell me about the people who influenced

you the most as a child

Question 24

What did you dream to be as a grown up?

Tell me how you imagined your future

when you were a child

Teens

Question   25

What high school did you go to?

Tell me what kind of student you were as

a teenager

Question 26

Were you part of any clubs?

Tell me about any sports or social

activities you would take part in

Question 27

What kind of music did you like?

Tell me some of your favorite songs or

singers and bands of that time

Question 28

When did you first drive a car?

Tell me how you learned to drive and

what car you would drive

Question 29

Did you get along with your parents?

Tell me how was your relationship with your parents during those years

Question 30

Who was your best friend?

Tell me how you would normally hang out with your friends

Question 31

Did you have a crush on someone?

Tell me about the first time you fell in

love in your teenage years

Question 32

What is your most embarrassing
memory?

Tell me about something awkward that
happened to you as a teenager

Question 33

Who did you look up to as a teenager?

Tell me about someone you particularly

admired during those years

Question 34

Did you enjoy being a teenager?

Tell me what kind of things you liked

doing or not so much as a teenager

Question 35

Were you outgoing?

Tell me what kind of personality you had

as a teenager

Question 36

What did you want to do after graduating?

Tell me how you were envisaging your future as an adult

Adulthood

Question 37

Did you go to college?

Tell me how you gained your professional

skills

Question 38

What was your first job?

Tell me how you moved out from your

parents' home

Question 39

Did you like your job?

Tell me what was your favorite and least

favorite job(s) you have done

Question 40

Where was your first adult home?

Tell me how you felt about settling into

your own home

Question 41

What was a memorable trip?

Tell me about the most adventurous

journey or vacation you had

Question 42

Where's your favorite place in the world?

Tell me what place is particularly special to you

Question 43

How did you fall in love?

Tell me how you met your partner

Question 44

When did you get married?

Tell me how was your wedding

Question   45

Do you have long lasting friendships?

Tell me which friends have mattered the

most to you

Question 46

Do you have any regrets?

Tell me what things you would change if

you could go back in time

Question 47

Have you changed much?

Tell me how you have evolved as an adult

Question 48

What's the most important life skill?

Tell me what skill or ability has helped

you the most to get through in life

Parenthood

Question 49

How old were you when you had children?

Tell me how the decision to have kids happened to you

Question 50

Did you always want to start a family?

Tell me what were your expectations and desires before having children

Question 51

How did you pick your children's names?

Tell me which other names you had

considered

Question 52

Were you hoping to have a son or a daughter?

Tell me some of your memories of the time you were expecting your first child

Question 53

How were the first days after the birth of your first child?

Tell me what were your first impressions as a new parent

Question 54

Was parenting easier or harder than you expected?

Tell me what were the most challenging and rewarding aspects about being a parent

Question 55

How did you choose your parenting style?

Tell me what was the best and worst

advice you were given on parenting

Question   56

If you could go back and change anything about being a parent, what would you do differently?

Question 57

What is a memory about your children that makes you laugh?

Tell me some funny story about my parents at that time

Question 58

How did you evolve as a parent?

Tell me how being a parent changed for you as your children grew older

Question 59

What did you pass on to your children?

Tell me what thing or aspect of yourself you find in your children

Question 60

What did parenthood mean to you?

Tell me something you have learned from

being a parent

Grand-parenthood

Question 61

How did you learn you were going to be a grandparent?

Tell me how you first found out and reacted to the news

Question 62

What's your favorite memory from when mom was expecting?

Tell me how you felt during that time and when I was first born

Question 63

Did you help name your grandchildren?

Tell me what other name you had wished

for your grandchildren

Question 64

How do you see yourself as a grandparent compared to other grandparents you know?

Question 65

What's the best thing about being a grandparent?

Tell me something new you have experienced as a grandparent

Question 66

Do you prefer being a grandparent to being a parent?

Tell me what is similar and different between being a parent and a grandparent

Question   67

What advice would you give on being a grandparent?

Question 68

Is there anything you want your grandchildren to have, or do, that you never did?

Question 70

What are your biggest hopes for your grandchildren's lives?

Question 71

Question 72

_____

Printed in Great Britain
by Amazon

33111593R00090